To Mark - 1999
Happy B...

D1623825

MARRIAGE
MOMENTS

MARRIAGE MOMENTS

*Heart-to-Heart Times
to Deepen Your Love*

David and Claudia Arp

VINE
BOOKS

SERVANT PUBLICATIONS
ANN ARBOR, MICHIGAN

Vine Books is an imprint of Servant Publications especially designed to serve evangelical Christians.

All Scripture quotations, unless indicated, are taken from the HOLY BIBLE, NEW INTERNATIONAL VERSION®. © 1973, 1978, 1984 by International Bible Society. Used by permission of Zondervan Publishing House. All rights reserved.

Published in association with the literary agency of Alive Communications, Inc., 1465 Kelly Johnson Blvd., Suite 320, Colorado Springs, CO 80920.

Published by Servant Publications
P.O. Box 8617
Ann Arbor, Michigan 48107

Cover design: Left Coast Design, Inc., Portland, OR
Cover photograph: Joe Carlson/Sharpshooters. Used by permission.

98 99 00 01 10 9 8 7 6 5 4 3 2 1

Printed in the United States of America

ISBN 1-56955-091-3

LIBRARY OF CONGRESS CATALOGING-IN-PUBLICATION DATA

Arp, Dave.
    Marriage moments : heart-to-heart times to deepen your love / David and Claudia Arp.
        p.   cm.
    Includes bibliographical references.
    ISBN 1-56955-091-3 (alk. paper)
    1. Marriage–Religious aspects–Christianity.   2. Spouses–Religious life.   I. Arp, Claudia.   II. Title
BV4596.M3A77   1998
242'.644–dc21   98-15318
                                                                 CIP

To all the couples who have participated
in our Marriage Alive Seminars. May you always
find "marriage moments" to deepen your love
for each other and for God.

Contents

Acknowledgments

To the many people who gave so much to this project, we wish to thank you for your support and encouragement. To Don Cooper, Bert Ghezzi, Gwen Ellis, Jeanne Mullins, Kathryn Deering, Greg Johnson, and the many others who helped us encourage couples to spend moments with each other and with God. We also thank all our sources, both known and unknown, whose influences have impacted our lives and allowed us to pass on this marriage message to others.

"My purpose is that they may be
encouraged in heart and united in love,
so that they may have the full riches
of complete understanding,
in order that they may
know the mystery of God, namely,
Christ, in whom are hidden
all the treasures of wisdom and knowledge."

COLOSSIANS 2:2-3

Before You Begin ...

Marriage is a wonderful mystery—a life drama in which husband and wife discover God's hidden treasures; "keeping themselves unto each other," they choose to make their marriage a promise for life. In a very real sense, an enriched Christian marriage reflects God's love to a world where, tragically, "starter" marriages are thrown away daily.

In the following pages we invite you to make your marriage a keepsake for life. To keep yourself unto each other means to honor, respect, sanctify and celebrate your marriage daily. In practical terms it means listening to your spouse when you'd rather go to sleep, hanging up the wet towel once again and even taking out the garbage. Putting your partner first through little daily acts of kindness, or mounting a concerted effort to replace negative habit patterns with positive ones, will help you treasure your marriage.

While habits are hard both to start and to break, we have discovered if we practice a desired habit for a month, we are well on the way to claiming it as our own. So for the next thirty-one days concentrate on making your marriage a treasured keepsake. Simply read one selection each day. Each chapter begins with a Scripture verse and encourages you to celebrate your marriage in a practical, concrete way.

Won't you join with us in this thirty-one-day adventure? In so doing, may you find hidden treasures and refreshment for the soul of your marriage.

David and Claudia Arp

Love Your
Closest Neighbor

Jesus replied, "'Love the Lord your
God with all your heart and with all
your soul and with all your mind.'
This is the first and greatest com-
mandment. And the second is like it:
'Love your neighbor as yourself.'"

MATTHEW 22:37–39

"There is no more lovely, friendly and charming relationship, communion or company than a good marriage."

MARTIN LUTHER

When Jesus was asked which is the great commandment, he responded with the top two: one, love God with all your heart, soul and mind; and two, love your neighbor as you love yourself. And it is when you love God with your heart, soul and mind that you are able to follow the second command to love your neighbor as yourself.

Just who is your neighbor? Loving your neighbor takes on a fresh, new meaning when applied to marriage. In the New Testament the key word, neighbor, means the person nearest and dearest to you. And if you are married, the person closest to you is your partner, the one with whom you chose to share life at its deepest and most intimate level.

How does this work out in daily life? If you love your partner as you love yourself, you will have his or her best interest at heart. You will want to serve, not be served, and you will resist the urge to manipulate or pull power plays. You will have a relationship based on love and trust.

So many times marital conflict would be resolved if you just loved the other as you love yourself. Too often we are "me" centered and want things to work out "my" way. But just the opposite approach is what promotes spiritual intimacy.

Take a few minutes and think of ways you can love your neighbor (your spouse). Consider the following ways to really love your partner:

- *Choose to really listen to your spouse.* Don't just think about how you are going to respond.

- *Look for ways to express your appreciation to your spouse.* You could make a top ten list of things you appreciate about your life partner.

- *Look for ways to serve, not be served.* When Dave goes out in the cold rain to get the paper and even lets Claudia have her favorite section first, he serves her. When Claudia relinquishes control of the remote and watches the football game with Dave, she serves him. When you agree to turn the lights off when you really want to keep on reading, you're being a servant.

Take our suggestions. Love God with all your heart, soul and mind, and love your spouse as you love yourself. Trust us. If you concentrate on loving your closest neighbor, your spouse, you'll demonstrate to a needy world that you love God also.

Master the Basics

"A man should fulfill his duty as a husband and a woman should fulfill her duty as a wife, and each should satisfy the other's needs."

1 CORINTHIANS 7:3 (TEV)

"Now this is the sum of the matter:
if ye will be happy in marriage,
confide, love and be patient;
be faithful, firm and holy."

MARTIN F. TUPPER

The creative task of marriage requires a day in, day out process of hard work and mutual adjustment. In a successful, growing marriage both the husband and the wife share their lives, support one another and continually seek to fulfill their duty to one another. But you've got to know the basics.

The good news is we know the skills that are needed in order to build an enriched marriage. The bad news is we don't always take the time to master them. Let's consider three basic essentials upon which we can build a healthy marriage:

1. The first basic essential is a deep commitment by both to share life in all its vital aspects "till death do us part." We're talking about permanence, but we're also talking about growth. You can have a lifelong commitment but, at the same time, have a dead relationship!

   Is your marriage growing and changing for the better? As we lead our Marriage Alive Seminar* around the country, sometimes people tell us, "We would come to your Marriage Alive Seminar, but we don't want to mess with our marriage." They are happy with the status quo, but God's plan for marriage is to grow closer to each other and to him as the years go by. And that requires a commitment to growth as well as permanence.

2. The second basic essential is honest, open communication. There's no room for being evasive or deceptive. Instead, it's essential to share how you really feel, to talk about your hopes, dreams and fears, knowing all the time that your expressed thoughts and feelings are safe.

   Here's a practical tip. When sharing how you feel, let the statement reflect back on you to avoid attacking your mate. Really pay attention to your spouse, both to the words and to the nonverbal message.

3. The third basic essential of a growing marriage is a willingness to deal with any issue that creates anger or disagreement. Face it, no one agrees on everything all the time. If we did, our marriage would certainly be boring! It will help to develop this basic skill if you agree not to attack each other or defend yourself so that you can focus on the issue at hand.

Take some time and talk about how you are doing in developing the basic essentials of commitment, communication and conflict resolution. The health and future of your relationship just may depend on mastering these basics.

* The Marriage Alive Seminar is a marriage education seminar designed to help couples revitalize their marriage. For more information see Seminars for Building Better Relationships in the back of this book.

Be Friends for Life

"There is a friend who sticks closer than a brother."

PROVERBS 18:24

"In survey after survey,
at least 80 percent of couples
in successful long-term relationships
report that they have become
best friends."

DR. GEORGIA WITKIN

I s your spouse your best friend? If so, you're on your way to having a great marriage. From the very first marriage to marriages today, friendship is a key factor in successful marriages.

Think about it. Have you ever met a couple on the way to the divorce court who were best friends? We haven't. So if being friends with your spouse is so important, what can you do today to build your friendship?

Daily we have the opportunity to deepen our friendship through spending time together; but we must do so intentionally or it just won't happen. So how can you foster quality time together?

According to psychologists Richard Matterson and Janis Long Harris, men and women have different friendship styles. Men value doing things together, while women value talking together. For that reason, shared activities and regular times to talk go hand in hand, allowing the friendship needs of each spouse to be met. But what can you do together? We've got some great suggestions for you.

From time to time we ask our Marriage Alive seminar participants how they are building their friendships. Here are some of their responses. (Note that all include talking and doing something together!)

- "We like to take the back roads, get lost and then find our way home again."

- "We work out together at the local gym."

- "We like to cook together. Lately, we've been learning to cook Chinese food."

- "We walk around the soccer field while our son practices soccer."

- "We took sailing lessons."

- "We do organic gardening."

- "On Saturday mornings we have a standing date to run errands together."

If we have whetted your appetite, make your own list of friendship-enhancing activities. Start by listing things you've done in the past that built your friendship. Then brainstorm things you would like to do in the future.

Remember to pick activities that include both talking and doing. Finding and nurturing shared interests and activities will nurture your friendship. And nurturing your friendship in marriage will help you stick together–closer than brothers!

Make an Anger Contract

"'In your anger do not sin':
Do not let the sun go down
while you are still angry."

EPHESIANS 4:26

"In every marriage
the two dynamic forces are love,
which seeks to draw the couple
together, and anger, which tends
to drive them apart."

DAVID MACE

Did you know that anger can energize your marriage? It's true, but you have to prepare beforehand. You can actually preempt a marital fight by learning how to handle disagreements and anger, before they occur.

Confusing? Not really. There's no better time to learn how to process anger than when you are calm, relaxed, away from all the pressures of life and not emotionally upset. So plan a time when you can be alone for a couple of hours.

Anger is a God-given emotion. It's our automatic response to fear and frustration. So anger isn't the problem; the problem is how you handle it. The Scriptures tell us to be angry yet not to sin and not to let the sun set on our anger. Since the sun goes down each day, anger is something that is not to linger. Instead we need to process it.

How can anger energize our marriage? Love and anger form a delicate balance in marriage. Love draws us together, and anger keeps us from losing our autonomy and becoming enmeshed! We don't have to worry about that, but we've had to learn how to balance love and anger by processing anger when it first appears.

We have decided that whatever issues arise, we will

agree not to attack each other or defend ourselves. From our mentors, Drs. David and Vera Mace, who initiated the marriage enrichment movement in Protestant churches, we learned how to make an anger contract. You can, too. Basically our anger contract has three parts. Whenever we become angry, we both agree to:

1. Acknowledge our anger to each other as soon as we become aware of it. This alerts the other that there is something we need to work out! Take a current situation at the Arps'. Claudia wants a neat bathroom, but often at night Dave's clothes end up draped over the side of the tub, not on a hanger. When Claudia sees them, rather than get "hot under the collar," she says, "Dave, I need to tell you I'm beginning to get angry." This lets Dave know something is bothering Claudia before she explodes in anger.

2. Then renounce the right to vent anger at each other or to defend ourselves. This helps us to avoid escalation and helps us focus on whatever is causing the anger. Claudia continues, "I'm getting angry, but I won't vent my anger on you."

3. Last, ask for each other's help in dealing with the anger that has developed. Together we can attack the problem, *not* each other, as in, "Dave, where could those clothes go rather than on the tub? Will you help me figure this one out?" The closet and the hamper are candidates, and with a hanger, the hook on the bathroom door is an option. Have we totally solved this one? No. Sometimes the clothes *still* end up on the tub, but we're attacking the *issue*, not each other.

A great time to talk about what you do when you get angry is when you're calm. Then talk about how you would like to respond the next time you are angry. Adopting our anger contract and agreeing not to attack each other or defend ourselves will make a huge difference the next time anger comes to visit.

Adopt this agreement and together, whatever the future holds, you can handle anger! And the sun can set on a harmonious note! Try it; it works for us.

Practice Love Talk

"Speaking the truth in love,
we will in all things grow up into
him who is the Head, that is, Christ."

EPHESIANS 4:15

"Language is the dress of thought."

SAMUEL JOHNSON

If you want to really communicate with your mate, you need to learn how to speak the truth in love. That rules out yelling and angry looks along with negative, attacking words.

Communicating the truth in love includes being willing to listen with love. And you must listen for the total message. "Why don't you listen to me?" is more than a trite question. Spouses in every stage and walk of life desperately desire to have their spouses listen to them. So why is listening so hard? And when we do listen, why do we so often misunderstand what the other person says?

One reason is that we are only listening to the words. And as important as the words are, they are only 7 percent of the total message! What you say is only a tiny part of the message. No wonder so many conversations are unheard dialogues. That's scary! If you don't understand the message, you'll have difficulty responding.

So what is the other 93 percent of the message? The tone of voice is 38 percent; how you say something is five times more powerful than what you say. So start listening for your tone of voice. That still leaves 55 percent of the message. And that's what you don't say in words–the shrugs, glares and all other nonverbal messages. We all know "the look."

Think about this: What message do you really give if

you say the right words, but your tone and look contradict them? Nothing devastates loving communication as much as a mixed message of loving words spoken in a bitter tone of voice! So as you listen to your spouse, also listen to your own message and make sure your words, nonverbal communication and tone of voice convey the same loving message.

Take a couple minutes and think of five unique ways to communicate your love to your mate without saying a word. For instance, Dave says "I love you" loudly and clearly when after dinner he leads Claudia to her favorite recliner, gives her an unread magazine, then disappears and becomes the "kitchen elf." Claudia says "I love you" when she sews that button on Dave's favorite shorts or when she puts on our favorite romantic music and gives Dave that "come hither" look.

Concentrate on expressing love to your spouse in actions as well as words. Then when you must speak the truth in love to confront other issues, your spouse just may hear and understand what you are saying.

In loving marriages and families, we say what we mean, mean what we say and look and sound like we mean it! Now, did you hear that?

Cultivate the Dating Habit

"I will betroth you to me forever;

I will betroth you in righteousness and justice,

in love and compassion.

I will betroth you in faithfulness,

and you will acknowledge the Lord."

HOSEA 2:19–20

"The husband found,
a lover is not lost,
The sweetheart still remains–
a sweetheart wife!"

S.C. HALL

Dating. Hey, that's what you did before marriage when you were betrothed. But if you want your marriage to go the distance, you need to continue to cultivate the dating habit! The commitment you made to each other when you chose each other for life will be enhanced and reinforced by the habit of dating.

How? First, dating gives you a format for spending quality time together. It's hard to energize your marriage when the kids are always around or the phone is ringing or the e-mail is beeping and you are never alone with your mate!

Second, dates–even short, inexpensive ones–renew your friendship. When you date, you make your spouse a priority, and that helps you keep your vow to love and cherish each other.

Have we convinced you that dating is beneficial? Then pull out your calendar. Choose a weekly date night and schedule a date. Then mark it "marriage priority time." Guard your date night with your life and if absolutely necessary, keep rescheduling until it happens.

"But you don't know our situation," one young mom told us.

"Oh yes, we do," we responded. "We remember what it

was like at our house when our boys were young, and that's why you have to make your marriage a high priority by dating your spouse."

Cultivating the dating habit will enrich your relationship for a lifetime. It takes three weeks to develop a new habit and six weeks to feel good about it. In no time at all, you can make your marriage a higher priority.

Since the dating habit is worth developing, why not make a date to plan more dates with your mate? Together make a list of fun dates you would both enjoy, anything from rock climbing, to taking a class together, to planning a romantic getaway for two. Then write your next date with your mate in your calendar. It's the first step in cultivating the dating habit and will remind you why you chose to betroth each other forever. (This could be so good for your marriage that we suggest you put this book down and find your calendar right now!)

Become Soul Mates

"And in him you too are being built together to become a dwelling in which God lives by his Spirit."

EPHESIANS 2:22

"In marriage reverence is
more important even than love …
A steady awareness in each that the
other has a kinship with the eternal."

FULTON J. SHEEN

Do you want to build intimacy with your spouse? Then together seek to build intimacy with God. You will discover that developing spiritual intimacy can enhance the overall quality of your marriage. You can become soul mates.

When we use the term "spiritual intimacy," we're talking about your core beliefs and how they affect who you are and what you do. Your core beliefs influence all dimensions of your life and are played out daily in the values you choose and the choices you make.

For us, being spiritually intimate is having a shared purpose in life–a mutual calling from God to something that is bigger than us. Our spiritual unity in Christ sees us through life's storms and gives us inner peace in the midst of a turbulent world.

We are convinced that having a spiritual dimension in marriage actually increases marital satisfaction. Research says we are right! Did you realize that couples who frequently pray together are twice as likely to describe their marriages as highly romantic and that those who are religious are less likely to divorce, have higher levels of satisfaction and higher levels of commitment?

It makes sense to us. Having a common faith in the

Lord will bind you together in the midst of dealing with problems and daily living and loving.

Why not plan an evening to talk about how you can build more spiritual intimacy in your marriage? Here are some questions to use as a catalyst:

- Where am I on my spiritual journey?

- What are some of the milestones in my walk with God so far?

- If one looked at my life, what would he or she surmise are my core beliefs about life, death, family, marriage and so on?

- In what ways are we spiritually intimate?

- What spiritual disciplines would we like to develop?

- How can we serve others together?

Perhaps you would like to choose one book to read together on a topic related to spiritual growth and commitment. Maybe you want to be more diligent about finding time to pray together or read the Scriptures together. Start today to concentrate on building spiritual intimacy with your spouse. Not only will you grow closer to each other, you will also grow closer to God.

Spell Love
"T-I-M-E"

"But I trust in you, O Lord;

I say, 'You are my God.'

My times are in your hands."

PSALM 31:14–15

"Time goes, you say? Ah no!
Alas, Time stays, we go."

HENRY DOBSON

The greatest hindrance to our dating life is writing books on dating. We get so busy helping other couples date and improve their marriages that we neglect investing time in our own relationship. Yet we know a prerequisite for a great marriage is investing daily in that four-letter word, T-I-M-E! Time is our most precious commodity. Really, when you think about it, time is more valuable to a marriage than money. So how can you make time for your marriage?

You can start by placing all your time in God's hands. Ask your heavenly Father to show you how to be a good steward of your daily allotment of time. We each have twenty-four hours a day, no more, no less. But we know firsthand how hard it is to find time for each other. Thank goodness, it's just *hard*, not impossible! Consider the following time finders:

- *Tag other activities.* Are you going to a couples' Bible study this week? Leave an hour earlier or come home an hour late. Voilà! You've just found sixty minutes to invest in your marriage!

- *Find time even when you're too tired to talk.* Who says you always have to talk to build your relationship? After the children are in bed, don't talk. Don't do anything but cuddle on the couch. Enjoy the inexpressible joy that comes from feeling loved and safe with each other. The next morning, you'll be amazed at the couple chatter. We have been!

- *Plan a middle-of-the-night adventure.* For the really adventuresome, set the alarm for the middle of the night, or from time to time get up an hour earlier than normal to talk and pray together.

- *Leave the TV off for twenty-four hours.* Or if you're really courageous, leave it off for a week or a month! If there is a national crisis, you'll hear about it soon enough. Spend the time you would have spent watching television talking with your mate.

- *Drive past the video store without stopping.* While it's fun now and then to relax by watching a movie, videos can become habit-forming and steal communication time. So the next time you're tempted to stop at the video store on the way home, don't. You've just freed up another evening!

You may never "find" the time to work on your marriage, but trust us, you can *make* the time–especially if first you place all of your time in God's hands. Now we're going to turn off our computer, put down our pens and invest some time in us.

Take Marital Vitamins

"Rejoice in the Lord always.
I will say it again: Rejoice!"

PHILIPPIANS 4:4

"The secret of a happy marriage
is simple:
Just keep on being as polite to one
another as you are to your friends."

R. QUILLEN

Our secret for a happy marriage? Practice preventive medicine by nurturing a spirit of rejoicing, looking for the positive and treating your spouse like a friend. In the process you'll be giving your mate marital vitamins!

Concentrating on the positive seems so simple, but anyone who has tried to do so knows, it's not that simple. But it is very effective. So add that extra touch of health to your marriage by giving each other marital vitamins. What's a marital vitamin? It's anything we do to encourage our mate. Just showing kindness and being considerate of each other can add to your marital health!

Our friend, Joe, literally gave his wife marital vitamins. He bought thirty empty capsules, typed out thirty compliments for his wife and put one in each capsule. On the bottle he wrote, "Take one a day for encouragement."

Dave tried to do this. "I actually went to a pharmacy and asked for empty capsules. The pharmacist stared at me like I was a drug dealer, so I quickly left without my marriage vitamin capsules! I had to come up with another idea so I folded little pieces of paper and put them in a jar."

Claudia's response: "They worked!"

Everyone needs encouragement. It's got to start somewhere, so why not with you? Take a couple of minutes right now to make a list of ways you can build up and encourage your mate. Start with these daily marriage vitamins:

- *Hugs:* Give lots of them!

- *Kisses:* Always kiss good morning and good night.

- *Secret signals:* Come up with your own. For us squeezing the hand three times means "I love you." Four squeezes means "I love you back."

- *Silly notes:* Put them in each other's lunches.

- *A little gift:* Give one for no reason at all.

- *Little surprises:* Pick up your mate's favorite candy bar.

- *Encouraging e-mail messages:* During the day send an e-mail message to say, "Hi, honey, I just wanted to let you know how much I love and appreciate you!"

Any of these vitamins will help you affirm your love and commitment to each other. So take a few minutes and make your own list of marriage vitamins. Let us give you this warning: marriage vitamins are habit-forming, but they can be very beneficial to your marital health.

Appreciate Your Hectic Heritage

"Sons are a heritage from the Lord,

children a reward from him."

PSALM 127:3

"A married couple who love their home, their family and their friends, create a charmed circle and make a warmth which radiates on all it touches."

MARY MACAULAY

Enriching your marriage while parenting your children may sound like an oxymoron, but not only is it possible, it's one of the greatest gifts you can give to your children.

The good news is your role as partner does not have to compete with your role as parent. However, balancing your roles requires much skill and may leave you tired just thinking about it! It helps to realize the ways your children enrich your marriage.

- *Children are a continual reminder that you are one.* Each time you see your daughter's big smile it reminds you of that smile that won you over years ago! What characteristics of your child's appearance or personality remind you of your spouse? Stop for a moment and reflect on your first pregnancy. Do you remember the hopes and dreams you had as you began your family?

- *Children foster teamwork and creativity.* Since children present many obstacles to finding time alone together, you have to get creative. Think about it–romance thrives on obstacles. Before we were married, we worked hard to overcome obstacles. We were at different universities two hours apart; nonetheless, most weekends we found ways to get together. What are the obstacles you presently need to overcome? Is it next to impossible to find sitters or to go on a date? Do your children strain your budget? How can you creatively make ends meet? How can you find little bits of time to invest in your marriage?

ᐣ *Children promote appreciation.* Because it's a challenge to make time for each other, you appreciate it more when you do get together. Reflect on some of the good times you have had together in the midst of parenting pressures. What qualities are magnified in your spouse as he or she parents your children? Claudia has always appreciated Dave's good sense of humor with our three sons, and Dave especially likes Claudia's creativity with our grandchildren.

So the next time you're tempted to see your children as obstacles to building your marriage, instead take some time to list the ways they enrich it! And one way you will enrich your own children is passing down to them a godly heritage. In families, we are all blessed, and through our families, we bless others as well!

Deal With the Gnats and Camels

"You strain out a gnat but swallow a camel."

MATTHEW 23:24

"Small to great matters
must give way."

WILLIAM SHAKESPEARE

W hat irritates you more, the little irritations or the big issues you face in your marriage? For us it's usually the little things. Sometimes we refer to them as "little gnats" in the soup; they aren't life-threatening, just irritating. Dealing effectively with the little gnats in our marriage helps us save some energy to deal with the larger camels of life. So what can you do to swat them out before they learn to swim?

Identify the gnats that keep coming up in your relationship. Sometimes we get upset over insignificant things such as:

- *Thermostat:* Your mate would make a good Eskimo and keeps turning the thermostat down, while you would like the house to be as warm as the tropics.

- *Attitude:* You are Mr. Positive and are married to Mrs. Negative or vice versa.

- *Toilet Paper:* You like the toilet paper to unroll from the top, but your mate likes it to unroll from the bottom or doesn't like it on the toilet paper holder at all!

- *Punctuality:* Your middle name is Punctuality, but your mate's name is Late Arriver.

- *Neatness:* You like that homey, lived-in look, but your mate arranges the magazines on the table at forty-five degree angles.

- *Toothpaste:* You are a precision toothpaste roller, but your mate is a creative squeezer.

If little things don't make sparks fly, big issues such as finances, children and priorities can ignite conflict. Whatever the issue, the key is to nurture a sense that you are working together against the problem and not against each other.

Take a gnat and camel checkup. Answer and discuss the following two questions:

1. What are the little gnats in your relationship? Those are the little irritations like leaving the daily newspaper on the floor or not putting dirty dishes in the sink.

2. What are the camels in your relationship? These are the larger issues that you need to address which might include agreeing on family size, making life style choices and deciding on careers.

As an action point, choose one irritation (gnat) and one issue (camel) to work on together. Work together to drown those little gnats before they learn how to swim and spoil your marital soup! Then you'll have more energy to stomp out the larger camels before they stomp you. This is one confrontation you can both win.

DAY TWELVE

Get Away

"May he give you the desire
of your heart
and make all your plans succeed."

PSALM 20:4

"Leisure is those periods when daydreaming is legitimate."

WARREN GOLDBERG

W ant to get away from pressures of life and put some fun in your relationship? Then plan a couple getaway! Over the years our relationship has been enhanced by times away from home. When our children were young, getaways were a wonderful break from our parenting responsibilities and hassles at home and gave us time to focus on each other.

Sometimes our getaways go like clockwork. Other times, they don't. Like when we were living in Germany and planned a weekend at a wonderful farmhouse bed-and-breakfast in the Black Forest. Our room came complete with a feather bed and a balcony overlooking the cattle grazing in the meadow and the mountains in the distance. That evening we had dinner at a lovely, out-of-the-way German restaurant and talked and talked, totally unconscious of the time. Little did we know that the farmer locked the doors at 10:00 P.M. When we got back to the farmhouse, our room key would not open the outside door and the farmer had gone to bed! So for our romantic getaway, we slept in our Volkswagen camper! Disappointing, to say the least!

Since other times were met with more success, we keep on planning getaways and encouraging other couples to do the same. No one debates the benefits of getting off alone with one's mate. But how can you get away for your getaway? The following planning guide can help you act on your good intentions. Together work through the following list:

1. *Places where you would like to go:* Make a list and then choose one.

2. *Resources for your getaway:* Work out a budget; is this getaway going to be economy, moderate or five-star? If funds are limited, borrow someone else's home or condominium, clip coupons or take your own food to save money. Open a special getaway account and save up for one.

3. *Possible dates:* Choose a date and write it in your calendar; also pick an alternate date in case things don't work out for the first one.

4. *Arrangements to make:* Make reservations, get maps, stop the newspaper and find child care. If you feel your children are just too young, remember that making

your marriage a priority by getting away will benefit your kids. And kids are survivors; others can care for them for several days! If child care is a problem, swap children with friends or start a child-care cooperative with other families. Save up to hire a sitter or recruit relatives.

5. *Packing list:* Think about the things you want to take along like candles, music and snacks.

But what if your spouse just isn't interested in getting away? We hear that one a lot! If this is your situation, you could offer to do all the planning or plan the getaway around something you know your spouse enjoys. Ask for a getaway as a present, or if your mate likes surprises, kidnap him or her. You just may end up with a very happy hostage!

Time alone will infuse your relationship with fun, intimacy and romance. Go on and prove us right. Trust God to help make your plans a wonderful reality as you take some time to dream together.

Discover Your Marriage Assets

"Accept one another, then, just as Christ accepted you, in order to bring praise to God."

ROMANS 15:7

"Where there is love in the marriage,
    there is harmony in the home;
when there is harmony in the home,
    there is contentment in the
    community;
where there is contentment in the
    community, there is prosperity in
    the nations;
when there is prosperity in the
    nations, there is peace in the world."

CONFUCIUS

Nations war with each other because of intolerance, but intolerance isn't just an international liability. We can find plenty of it in our homes and in our marriages. We just label it differently. In fact, we've noticed in our relationship that many times lack of acceptance is at the root of our intolerance. Have you ever said, "My wife is just too disorganized," or, "My husband is such a pessimist"?

For marriage, intolerance is a real downer. How can we give our marriage a big dose of tolerance? A great start is to follow Paul's advice in Romans 15:7 to accept each other as Christ accepted us. And acceptance involves understanding your unique differences, not only tolerating them but actually seeing them as assets!

You can build a strong marriage by benefiting from each other's unique strengths. Yet we often react negatively when we see differences in each other, not considering those differences as couple assets.

Think with us for a moment. What attracted you to your spouse in the first place? Did the things that attracted you to each other before marriage become irritations after marriage? They did for us. When we first met, Claudia loved how Dave was so easygoing and was never in a hurry. Dave liked Claudia's endless energy. There was always something to do or some place to go. Just being around her was exciting.

Then we got married. All of sudden Claudia realized this man she had married wouldn't move! And it dawned on Dave that he had married Miss Activity, and all he wanted was a quiet evening at home. Right away we were confronted with our differences.

When we began to realize that the ways we are different gave balance, we began to tolerate and discover our marriage assets. You can make the same discovery. For example:

- The time-oriented spouse will help you stay on schedule, while the people-oriented spouse will help you be more sensitive to others.

- The spontaneous partner will interject fun and excitement into the relationship, and the organized planner will keep you from chaos!

- The night owl will be great at waiting up for that last teenager to get home, and the morning lark will be all sparkle with the baby at 5:00 A.M.

Take a few minutes and identify your couple assets. Answer these two questions:

1. What ways are you alike? How do you need to compensate? For instance, if both of you are planners, life could be mundane and boring. So from time to time one of you could plan a surprise for the other.

2. What ways are you different? Do you see ways you can benefit from your differences? In what areas do you need to be more tolerant? For instance, Claudia still doesn't understand why any sane person would ever want to take a nap in the middle of the day!

As you refocus, can you see your differences as potential assets? If so, you are on your way to claiming tolerance for your marriage. Keep looking for ways to complement each other, and you'll find that tolerance will become one of your greatest assets!

Give Your Marriage
Three Gifts

"Be imitators of God, therefore, as dearly loved children and live a life of love, just as Christ loved us and gave himself up for us as a fragrant offering and sacrifice to God."

EPHESIANS 5:1–2

"The goal in marriage is not to think alike, but to think together."

ROBERT C. DODDS

Do you ever find yourself in those situations when you simply cannot agree, even though you love God and each other? In a growing, alive marriage, conflict and disagreements are just part of the landscape.

Show us a marriage where spouses never disagree, and we'll show you a marriage that is stagnating! But too many marriages fall apart when partners lack skills to deal with the inevitable anger and conflict that every close relationship must face.

Our advice is to follow Paul's admonition in Ephesians 5:1 to live a life of love. Christ is our model. If we have his attitude of self-sacrifice in our marriage, dealing with disagreement will be easier.

If you are facing a situation right now and don't know where to start to resolve it, here's our tip: consider three gifts you can give to your marriage. One of them may be just right for the present situation.

1. *The gift of love: "Let's do it your way."* When an issue is more important to your spouse than to you, simply give a gift of love by saying, "This time, let's do it your way." A caution: A gift of love is a great gift which only works over the long haul if, at other times, the other spouse also gives love gifts.

2. *The gift of individuality: "We'll do it differently."* That's when we realize we don't have to agree on everything. It's fine sometimes just to agree to disagree and to maintain our separate perspectives about an issue. Maybe you like different styles of music or have different food preferences. After all, wouldn't it be boring if we agreed on everything!

3. *The gift of compromise: "We'll meet in the middle."* The third gift is when we both give a little to find some middle ground. And for us, this happens often. Take snack foods. Claudia would say, "Don't eat them!"; she looks for the "no fat, no taste" variety. Dave goes for "high fat." We compromise with "low fat, some taste."

Now let's get practical. Can you remember a time recently when you gave your partner a gift of love? Maybe you got up in the middle of the night to comfort a crying child or volunteered to return the phone messages. If you can't remember a recent gift of love, think of one you could give to your mate today.

When was the last time you resolved a difference by each giving a gift of individuality? Maybe you voted differently in the last election and chose not to make it an issue.

Have you recently given each other the gift of compromise? Maybe you're the miser and your spouse thinks money grows on trees, but on a recent purchase decision, you met in the middle.

Now look to the future. The next time you face conflict, remember our three gifts. Like us, you may discover that when you're committed to your marriage and you're willing to give love gifts of cooperation and compromise, your marriage will just get better.

Have Prayer Dates

"Devote yourselves to prayer, being watchful and thankful."

COLOSSIANS 4:2

"How beautiful is the marriage of two Christians, two who are one in hope, one in desire, one in the way of life they follow, one in the religion they practice.... They pray together, instructing one another, encouraging one another, strengthening one another."

TERTULLIAN

Prayer is a unique resource we have in a Christian marriage. God simply delights when couples pray. In *To Understand Each Other,* Paul Tournier writes that praying together is the highest tie binding a couple:

> *Happy are the couples who do recognize and understand that their happiness is a gift of God, who can kneel together to express their thanks not only for the love which he has put in their hearts, the children he has given them or all of life's joys, but also for the progress in their marriage which he brings about through the hard school of mutual understanding.*

Praying together is one of our most precious marriage keepsakes, but doing so hasn't always been easy. Frankly, when we first tried, it was a disaster! One of us was more verbal than the other—OK, it was Claudia. She would get "on a roll" and pray about this and then pray about that, and by the time she finished, all Dave could say was "Amen." Not a great couple prayer experience. However, we were determined so we didn't give up. Soon we learned to make a prayer list and to take turns praying short prayers. From time to time we have more extended times of prayer which we call our "prayer dates." Since this is a habit you might want to start, let us give you some tips:

- ٭ Start by reading the Scriptures together. This will help you get in tune with God and with each other. Share your favorite passages.

- ٭ Talk about how God has answered prayers in the past and how he has led you in your life, your family and your marriage.

- ٭ Make a prayer list and write down specific requests. You may even want to start a prayer log where you can later write in the answers!

- ٭ Make a list of things you agree to pray for each other and for each of your children. Keep this list in your Bible as a daily reminder.

- ٭ Remember to pray with each other.

Maybe you are thinking, "I'd love to have a prayer date, but my spouse is just not that far along in his or her spiritual journey." Then consider starting with the Quaker model of prayer, shared silence. This would allow you to worship God separately and privately, knowing that you are sharing the experience together. It's an easy first step in praying and worshiping together. (Now according to the Quaker tradition, you end your devotional time with a kiss of peace!)

Take the risk. Let your relationship with God foster closeness with your mate. Developing the habit of prayer, whether sharing silence, simply praying for each other or actually praying aloud together, will result in great and wonderful things as your heavenly Father hears and answers.

Build a Partnership

"Whatever you do, work at it with all your heart, as working for the Lord, not for men, since you know that you will receive an inheritance from the Lord as a reward."

COLOSSIANS 3:23–24

"Beloved, let us love so well,
Our work shall still be better
    for our love,
And still our love be sweeter
    for our work,
And both commended
    for the sake of each,
By all true workers and
    true lovers born."

ELIZABETH BARRETT BROWNING

How can you learn to partner together? Start by realizing that marriage is a calling from God. In the beginning God created us male and female, and from the beginning, his plan is that we will reflect his image to those around us as we love and partner together. Nothing reflects God's image in quite the same way as a loving, enriched Christian marriage where husband and wife are partners loving each other and harmoniously working together.

Maintaining a harmonious partnership happens to be a real challenge for us because we are continually together. We write together, we speak and lead seminars together, we even share an office with desks that face each other. We know we are the exception, but all couples need to be able to cooperate, share responsibility and work together. How are you doing with this challenge?

To evaluate your partnership, take a responsibility checkup. You will want to find a quiet place where you won't be interrupted, perhaps your favorite coffeehouse or ice cream shop. Take some paper and a pen. Then away from the kids and other distractions, talk about the ways you partner together. What are those areas in which you need to shore up your partnership? Consider the following:

- *Parenting:* What about your parenting responsibilities? If you're not united as parents, trust us, your children (especially in the adolescent years) will make mince-meat out of your yes's and no's.

- *Household responsibilities:* Divide and conquer lists help us partner together. (For tips on approaching your household "to-do" list, see Day Twenty-Four.)

- *Leisure activities:* Do you plan your fun times together? Who decides where you go for vacations?

- *Extended family:* More than one marriage has broken up under the stress of in-law and family pressures. How can you unite and work together in relating to your extended family?

- *Religious activities:* Do you choose together how and where you will worship God and serve others?

- *Financial issues:* Do you agree on financial decisions? What about short- and long-term savings? Retirement planning?

If your partnership is lopsided, with one making most of the decisions, it's time to go to work. You can learn to partner with your spouse and build a marriage that will reflect God's image as written in the first chapter of Genesis. Not only will God reward you, but *"[your] love [will] be sweeter for [your] work"* (Elizabeth Barrett Browning).

Wear a Marriage Preserver

"He replied, 'You of little faith, why are you so afraid?'

"Then he got up and rebuked the winds and the waves, and it was completely calm. The men were amazed and asked, 'What kind of man is this? Even the winds and waves obey him!'"

MATTHEW 8:26–27

"Sail forth into the sea of life,

O gentle, loving, trusting wife.

And safe from all adversity upon the

bosom of that sea

Thy coming and thy goings be!

For gentleness and love and trust

Prevail o'er angry wave and gust."

HENRY WADSWORTH LONGFELLOW

Someone aptly referred to marriage as the sea of matrimony because spouses have such a hard job keeping their heads above water. Can you identify? Are the winds and waves buffeting your marriage? At times do you feel you are drowning? Does everything but your marriage demand your time and attention? Does your work follow you home each evening? Are your children so demanding you have little time left over for you, much less your marriage? If you answered yes to any of these questions, it may be time for you to let God calm the storm and help you set marriage boundaries. They can be a real marriage preserver.

A marriage boundary is a defining line that says, "Stop! This time belongs to us!" We readily set boundaries to protect our productive time in our jobs and even to protect our family times, but we seldom think about setting boundaries for our marriages. Isn't it time to make some changes? We suggest the following steps:

1. *Identify present storms.* Are you too busy with your work or is your social calendar out of control? Are you struggling with your financial situation or with your relationship with your in-laws? Are friends demanding most of your free time? Do you need to establish some

new boundaries? For us, working in marriage education is good because the topic of marriage remains front and center, but bad because sometimes we tend to get so busy helping other couples, we neglect our own relationship. This brings us to the second step.

2. *Evaluate your marriage.* Talk about what's right about your marriage at present and areas where growth is needed. We try to set more time aside just for us, to designate times we will not talk about our work (even though our work deals with marriage!).

3. *Set marriage goals.* Write down both short- and long-term goals. Maybe you want to work on your communication skills, or maybe you want to start the habit of dating. Presently, we are working on establishing boundary lines between our work in marriage education and our own marriage, so one of our goals is to plan a getaway with one rule—we won't talk about our work, only about us!

4. *Learn new skills.* What skills do you need to learn that will help you make needed changes? Maybe you want to read a book on how to process anger and resolve conflict or learn new skills that will enhance your love life.

5. *Decide what you are not going to do!* As important as goal setting is, learn to say no. This is the bottom line of "boundary setting." No one is bionic. We aren't angels. We need to eat, sleep and rest. So be brutal and say no even to some good things that aren't the best for you or for your marriage.

6. *Take some action!* With boundaries now in place, take action on what is best for your marriage. Consider starting a dating club with other married couples so you will have positive peer pressure to keep working on your marriage and supportive couples' friendships to encourage you along the way.

We hope our suggestions will help, and that the next time you hear the term "boundaries" you will continue to set some for your marriage. They can help preserve your marriage, and you may even find that the winds and waves of life will calm down!

Adopt a Daily Sharing Time

"Love and faithfulness meet together;
righteousness and peace
    kiss each other.
Faithfulness springs forth
    from the earth,
and righteousness looks down
    from heaven."

PSALM 85:10–11

"Love is not just looking at each other, it's looking in the same direction."

ANTOINE DE SAINT-EXUPÉRY

D o you want to honor your commitment to your spouse? Then start the habit of having a daily sharing time. It will keep you communicating with each other, and it only takes ten minutes!

We can give a personal testimony, crediting our friends and mentors, Drs. David and Vera Mace, who encouraged us years ago to start the ten-minute daily sharing time. (Of course, you can extend the time whenever you want.)

The Maces suggested having our sharing time at a regular time each day. For them, the best time was first thing in the morning over a cup of tea. Our sharing time occurs when we walk for our health–a great exercise for the health of our marriage too. We love to walk outside, but when the weather doesn't permit, we head for the local shopping mall. We go *before* the stores open so we focus on each other, save money and don't get side-tracked. To have your own daily sharing time, claim ten minutes, take a walk or sit down with a cup of coffee and talk about these four questions:

1. How are you feeling now about what has happened to you since your last sharing time?

2. Is anything troubling you?

3. What plans do you have for the next twenty-four hours?

4. Are you aware of any issue in our relationship about which we need to talk? If so, when can we schedule a time to talk about it?

Your questions from day to day may vary, but the important point is to stay in touch emotionally with each other and to share about experiences that affect your relationship. If you want, you can read the Scriptures and pray together. Our couple walks provide a great time for prayer. You'll start your day better connected to each other and to God.

Let us encourage you to take the Maces' and the Arps' advice. Start a daily sharing time. We promise that you'll share more good times together.

Stick Together

"For this reason a man will leave his father and mother and will be united to his wife, and they will become one flesh."

GENESIS 2:24

"We are all angels with but one wing.

We fly only when we embrace."

LEO BUSCAGLIA

In the first book of the Bible we are given the secret for making marriages last. Genesis 2:24 challenges us to leave our homes and families of origin, cleave to each other and become one. Cleaving gives the picture of sticking together, both in easy times and hard times. It's joining wings and permanently flying together!

So if you would like to divorce-proof your marriage, stick together. Apply the Genesis 2:24 marital super glue. Did you realize that about half of all divorces occur in the first three to five years of marriage? Unfortunately, today, some view their marriages as "starter marriages" similar to starter homes. How tragic!

What can we do to insure that our marriage does not become a divorce statistic? In searching for that elusive glue that holds a marriage together, we found some common characteristics of marriages that are following the leave and cleave principle. While there are no perfect marriages, there are little things you can do that will help you stick together. Consider the following:

- *Be physical.* Touch your partner in an affectionate way each day. Tell your spouse, "I need a hug!" Try kissing each other for five seconds each time you say hello and good-bye. We started this habit, and we were surprised how long five seconds can be when you're kissing! It's enough to slow you down and focus on each other.

- *Set aside some time each day to talk.* Even if it's only a few minutes each morning and evening, talking will help you feel connected to each other. We have to admit talking daily is more critical to Claudia than to Dave, but it's vital for our relationship. So whoever has the greatest need can be the initiator.

- *Talk honestly.* Talk about issues that create tension, but try to avoid strong criticism, shouting and anger. Remember you are partners and you want to help and support each other.

- *Pray together daily.* Praying together is a great marital glue. It's hard to pray together if there is tension in your relationship. Keep short accounts with each other and also with God.

➥ *Plan fun times together.* Don't feel guilty when you leave your children to have fun with your mate. You are modeling a healthy and growing marriage that will impact future generations.

➥ *Say it often.* Lastly, communicate often, both verbally and nonverbally, "Honey, I'm sticking with you."

Why not take a few minutes and make a list of ways you can cleave to each other? What are the kinds of activities that glue you together? Try to accelerate those things and minimize the things that tend to pull you apart.

Take our tips. Divorce-proof your marriage. Remember, if you want to stick together, a super marriage holds together with this kind of glue: hugs ... touches ... conversation ... and prayer.

Grow Wise
Together

"Is not wisdom found among the aged? Does not long life bring understanding?"

JOB 12:12

"Grow old along with me. The best is
   yet to be;
The last of life, for which the first was
   made.
Our times are in His hand who saith,
   'A whole I planned, Youth shows but
   half; Trust God: See all, nor be
   afraid.'"

ROBERT BROWNING

We've got great news! Contrary to popular opinion, you are never too old to grow wiser. So many times we get set in our ways and just assume we're too old or don't have the energy to make wise changes. However, the Scriptures tell us that both wisdom and understanding–which are attributes of the aged–enable us to make needed changes.

Research validates that we can continue to change throughout life. James Peterson, a researcher at the University of Southern California who headed up a major study on aging, said one of the most exciting things he discovered is that old people can change their behavior up to the day of their death. If you feel you're already set in your ways and cannot change, you're wrong. It is never too early or too late to make wise changes for the better to ensure marital success. You can renew your zest for your partner and can look to the future with hope.

Start by reviewing your marriage history. How have you changed in the past to keep your marriage alive and growing? In the past decade our life changed drastically. Our three sons married and became parents, which made us grandparents. It seems only yesterday that we were in the toddler stage of family life, and now we have an empty nest. Where are you in your life? You may want to take a few minutes and reflect on the following questions:

- What is changing in your life right now?

- What new pressures do these changes put on your relationship with your spouse?

- What changes do you need to make at the present time? Small adjustments made now can make a tremendous difference in where your marriage goes in the future.

- Looking to the future, what changes might you need to make? Is the empty nest on the horizon? Maybe your nest has emptied only to refill with adult children or aging parents.

- What changes will retirement bring? We chuckle at the wife who candidly told us, "I married Ralph for life but not for lunch!" She wasn't laughing.

Wherever you are in your life, you're probably experiencing changes. Here are four tips to help you grow old wisely:

1. Realize change and growth in marriage are healthy.

2. Revise your expectations. Embrace change.

3. Don't sacrifice growth for stability. Coexistence is not growth!

4. Be willing to try new things.

Take a few minutes and think of just one way you would like to change that will make your marriage better. Maybe it's something as simple as helping with the dishes, taking out the garbage or calling more often to say, "I was just thinking about you and wanted to tell you how much I love you."

Take our advice. Do one thing today to enhance your relationship, and then along with Robert Browning you can wisely say, "Grow old along with me. The best is yet to be."

Spread a Little Joy

"Each one should use whatever gift he has received to serve others, faithfully administering God's grace in its various forms.... If anyone serves, he should do it with the strength God provides, so that in all things God may be praised through Jesus Christ."

1 PETER 4:10–11

"The goal of life should not be to find joy in marriage, but to bring more love and truth into the world. We marry to assist each other in this task."

LEO TOLSTOY

The Scriptures tell us it is more blessed to give than to receive. When you serve others, the greatest blessing may be yours! Together discovering the joy of doing something for someone else can be a real marriage enricher. First, you'll learn more about each other as you work together on a project. Second, serving others without thought of a reward or recognition can enrich your marriage relationship. As you focus together on helping others, you'll stop focusing on getting things "your way."

If we have convinced you, look around your community. Survey the needs and together choose a service project. Following is a list of possible projects. Use it as a catalyst to come up with your own unique brand of service.

1. Help build a house for Habitat for Humanity.

2. Volunteer for a short-term service project.

3. Adopt a missionary family. Remember birthdays and anniversaries with small gifts.

4. Volunteer to team teach Sunday school.

5. Choose an ecology project like starting a neighborhood recycling program.

6. Be an aunt and uncle to a child in a single-parent home.

7. Give financial support and practical help to a needy family.

8. Help an elderly neighbor with special needs such as providing transportation, shopping or just being available to talk.

We believe shared service promotes spiritual intimacy in a marriage relationship and is one way you can bring glory and honor to God. In *Kingdoms in Conflict,* Chuck Colson writes about the church having little Christian outposts in a world that desperately needs hope. As we serve others together, we can become little beacons that give light to others and create a thirst for God.

Why not take a few minutes and reflect on how you can spread a little joy to others!

Find More Hours in Your Day

"Come to me, all you who are weary and burdened, and I will give you rest. Take my yoke upon you and learn from me, for I am gentle and humble in heart, and you will find rest for your souls. For my yoke is easy and my burden is light."

MATTHEW 11:28–30

"So many worlds, so much to do,
so little done, such things to be."

ALFRED, LORD TENNYSON

Do you need more hours in your day? Are you weary? If you are married with children, your answer is undoubtedly "yes." Weary and tired may seem like a permanent part of life's landscape, yet our heavenly Father promises rest to those who come to him. He gives us spiritual refreshment and helps us renew our perspective. We may not find more hours in the day, but with his help we can look for ways to slow the pace. If you feel life is getting out of control and time for building a better marriage relationship is missing, it may be time to slow down. And here are some tips for doing just that!

- *Move your children's bedtime up by thirty minutes.* Your kids may not be enthusiastic, but if you hold your ground, you just may find more time to invest in your marriage.

- *Grab time for two.* Older children can understand that Mom and Dad need time alone. They may not jump up and down with excitement, but you can establish a time when they realize you don't want to be disturbed. When our three sons were teenagers, we remodeled our bedroom and added a sitting area so we had a place to escape! When our door was closed, it meant, "Stay out!" And to make sure they did when we really wanted privacy, we would lock our door.

- *Stop competing with Heloise and Martha Stewart.* Look for shortcuts. For instance, to make cutout cookies with your preschooler, start with a roll of refrigerated cookie dough! With fun shapes and sprinkles they'll look and taste homemade. You can make great homemade pizza with frozen crust already rolled out. Homemade bread can start with frozen dough.

- *Simplify your routines.* Are mornings hectic at your house? When you need a break, let your children sleep in their sweats; the next morning they are already dressed and ready to go!

- *Recruit some help.* Do you dread that arsenic hour right before dinner? Hire an older neighborhood kid to play with or read to your little ones while you collect your wits and prepare dinner.

🍃 *Say no.* When you feel overwhelmed, and you are about to add another commitment to an already too busy schedule, pull out that little two-letter miracle word "no!"

Trust us, these ideas will help you slow the pace. You'll enjoy your marriage just a little bit more, and you may find your daily burden is not so heavy!

Make Marriage a Threesome

"Two are better than one, because they have a good return for their work: If one falls down, his friend can help him up. But pity the man who falls and has no one to help him up!

"Also, if two lie down together, they will keep warm. But how can one keep warm alone?

"Though one may be overpowered, two can defend themselves. A cord of three strands is not quickly broken."

ECCLESIASTES 4:9–12

"There's a bliss beyond all
    that the minstrel has told,
When two that are link'd
    in one heavenly tie,
With heart never changing
    and brow never cold,
Love on through all ills,
    and love on till they die!"

THOMAS MOORE

A Christian marriage is a threesome. The husband, the wife and God. Picture three individual strands woven together to make a cord of great strength–that's a word picture of an enriched, successful Christian marriage.

Our shared faith in Jesus Christ gives us a common focus in life. Our Christian faith is simply foundational to our having an enriched, healthy marriage. Sharing a common belief system gives us the opportunity to develop spiritual intimacy with each other. Thousands of years ago, King Solomon saw the value of spiritual intimacy when he said, "Two are better than one, because they have a good return for their work.... [And even better,] a cord of three strands is not quickly broken" (Eccl 4:9, 12).

Many times we let each other down, and that's when we look to our third strand to help us keep our marriage vows. Our strands were frayed very quickly when we were facing an international move. Dave thought it was the greatest opportunity and adventure of a life. But Claudia thought it was a disastrous idea that would be the biggest mistake of our lives! Without our common faith in Christ and his leadership in this decision, Dave might have gone to Europe and Claudia might have stayed in Tennessee.

Our strands would not even have been on the same continent!

In the end we did move to Germany. It wasn't one of the best of times in our marriage, but our relationship with Christ during this period helped us keep our cords intertwined. Things got better, and God used the difficulties we experienced in those years to lead us to our present work as marriage and family life educators!

Ecclesiastes 4:9-12 became our special marriage passage. Today when we begin to pull in different directions, we come back to the biblical picture of marriage as a cord of three strands. Through this Scripture, God renews our perspective.

Do you have a marriage verse? If not, we suggest you search the Scriptures and find a passage that you could claim for your marriage. Maybe you will want to adopt our Ecclesiastes passage. As Christians, the Bible is a wonderful resource in helping us build better relationships. Your marriage can be marked by a joyful spirit, surrounded by the peace of God and his presence when you allow him to be the third strand.

Take Out
the Garbage

"Serve wholeheartedly, as if you were
serving the Lord, not men, because
you know that the Lord will reward
everyone for whatever good he does,
whether he is slave or free."

EPHESIANS 6:7–8

"If a task is once begun

Never leave it till it's done.

Be the labor great or small

Do it well or not at all."

ANONYMOUS

"Isn't it time somebody took out the garbage?" is more than a trite question, at least at our house. Tuesday is the day the garbage collector comes to our neighborhood. Monday night is garbage stress time, especially when we forget about it until we are snug in bed.

What are those chores at your house that test your teamwork? One stress common to marriage is completing all the chores. What a difference it might make if we took Paul's good advice to serve one another whether we are slaves or free! And from time to time don't we all feel we are "slaving" for each other? If you're feeling that way right now, it's time to have a talk!

Why not have a marriage powwow and divvy up your household chores? You can cut down on disagreements and free up more time for doing the things you enjoy.

When deciding who will do what, it's helpful to consider how often each task needs to be done. Meal preparation is daily; paying bills may be monthly. We suggest making a list of the tasks that need to be done. Everybody's list will be different, but to get you started here are some common areas:

- doing the laundry
- meal preparation
- kitchen cleanup
- vacuuming and dusting
- cleaning the bathrooms
- household repairs
- paying the bills and balancing the checkbook
- grocery shopping
- correspondence
- yard work
- car maintenance
- carpools, homework, sports practices and so on.

Talk about your present responsibilities. If you are not sharing the load equitably, forget who does what and start over. Divide up the jobs. Start by choosing those things you enjoy doing; then tackle those jobs that nobody wants to do. Maybe you can take turns or attack some of the big ones together.

Negotiate until you both feel you've got a plan you can live with. Don't overlook those you could recruit to help (your children and outside help). And yes, decide whose chore it is to take out the garbage. That alone will be a great marriage keeper!

"Wise Up" Your Marriage

"Do not forsake wisdom, and she will protect you; love her, and she will watch over you.

Wisdom is supreme; therefore get wisdom.

Though it cost all you have, get understanding.

Esteem her, and she will exalt you; embrace her, and she will honor you."

PROVERBS 4:6–8

"A happy marriage is a long conversation that always seems too short."

ANDRÉ MAUROIS

What does a wise marriage look like? Picture a couple who freely and openly talk to and understand one another. They observe each other and are sensitive to what is said and what is unsaid. That's wisdom.

It's easy to get in a rut of shallow conversations, not really listening to each other or noticing the other person's mood. How can you become a wise observer? Start by upgrading your communication skills.

Recently we upgraded our computers. We deleted unneeded files and added new features to help us be more efficient. Frankly, it was a little scary, but now we love our more powerful computers and would not go back to the old programs.

If your communication is like our old computer programs (working but not at its peak performance), then take our advice–upgrade it! And you do just that by learning new skills and retooling the ones you already know.

Upgrading your communication will make your marriage wise, but be prepared for some surprises and new insights. You may discover that:

    Wise communication is more than chatter. We all chitchat daily–from "How was your day?" to "Where's the remote?"—but if that's all you do, then you probably have a marriage that lacks warmth and depth. When you upgrade your communication, you will learn how to share your deeper feelings and have heart-to-heart talks that pull you closer together. So start telling your mate what you are really thinking and feeling.

❧ *Wise communication is nonattacking.* When we confront the issue and not each other, we build the relationship. Resist attacking the other or defending yourself. Then you can create a safe atmosphere in which you'll be more willing to share your true feelings with each other. Remember to start your sentences with "I" and let them reflect back on you. Avoid "Why" questions and "You" statements, which tend to be attacking and zap energy—and your marriage.

❧ *Wise communication is companionate communication.* What do we mean by "companionate" communication? It's going the extra mile to understand and really connect with each other, the kind of communication that builds your friendship. Really listening and expressing yourself in specific yet positive words will help you become close companions.

Upgrading your communication skills can open new opportunities for growth and intimacy. As you are in the process of learning new skills, remember to be honest, yet never unkind. You can be direct, yet positive. Remember, you're developing healthy skills that will enrich your marriage through all the conversations of your life. That's something all wise couples desire.

Be a Five-Star Lover

"My lover is mine and I am his."

SONG OF SONGS 2:16

"The attainment of sexual harmony is one of the tasks every married couple must undertake. It depends far less upon biological factors than upon those virtues of kindness, courtesy and consideration for others which should be cultivated by every Christian."

DAVID AND VERA MACE

Are you a five-star lover? If not, you can become one! Being a great lover involves much more than just the physical side of love. Your love life should encompass the totality of your relationship.

First, a great loving relationship begins with acknowledging that you belong exclusively to each other. Your spouse is your love gift from your heavenly Father, and you are to "keep yourself unto him or her as long as you both shall live."

Second, a great lover is other-centered. He seeks to serve the other. She is kind, courteous and considerate. As Solomon's beloved said it so well in the Song of Songs, "My lover is mine and I am his" (2:16), and your goal should be to please each other.

Third, a five-star lover, like a multifaceted diamond, demonstrates the many dimensions of love. What do you think of when you think of sex? Most men tend to think of physical closeness, while most women tend to think of emotional closeness. Both are components of a five-star love life, but a great love life includes other facets such as: trust–feeling safe with each other; mutuality–freely choosing to love each other; honesty–openly communicating your true feelings; and pleasure–giving joy to each other. All work together to create an atmosphere of romance and intimacy, which is a great setting for becoming a five-star lover.

So how is your love life? What are the best aspects and what areas would you like to work on? From our national "Love, Sex, Kids, and Marriage" survey, we learned what couples considered the best aspects of their love life. While the responses were varied, several themes emerged as essential components for a five-star loving relationship.

You may want to talk about how you are doing in these areas:

- A five-star lover puts his or her spouse first and seeks to bring pleasure to the other.

- A five-star lover dares to be always truthful but never unkind.

- A five-star lover affirms absolute loyalty to his or her mate.

- A five-star lover sacrifices for his or her spouse.

🍃 A five-star lover energizes the relationship with fun and laughter.

To these we would add:

🍃 A five-star lover says often, "Hey, let's have a date!"

🍃 When your mate asks for a date, a five-star lover responds, "YES!"

A five-star lover understands the components of love: trust, mutuality, honesty, pleasure and intimacy. Just talking about how you can be a better lover will energize your relationship. This is one conversation with a long-term payoff!

Adapted from our book *Love Life for Parents* (Grand Rapids, Mich.: Zondervan, 1998), chap. 2, "What's a Love Life?"

Be Partner-Focused

"Do nothing out of selfish ambition or vain conceit, but in humility consider others better than yourselves. Each of you should look not only to your own interests, but also to the interests of others."

PHILIPPIANS 2:3–4

"The 'wilt thou' answer'd and again

The 'wilt thou' asked,

till out of twain

Her sweet 'I will' has made you one."

ALFRED, LORD TENNYSON

The two shall become one. In a healthy, alive marriage partners complement each other and experience a unique oneness. We still are complete individuals; we still care about others, our careers, our family and our friends, but continually we must choose to focus on each other.

Where are you in the process of becoming partner-focused?

- *Are you newlyweds?* Are you just beginning to learn how to unselfishly focus on each other? It's easy to continue to think "single," but in an alive marriage, the focus is on "togetherness." Good relationship habits formed now will enrich your marriage in the years ahead.

- *Are you in the active parenting years?* Are you in the energy crunch of parenting toddlers or adolescents? While sharing the parenting load, are you reserving time for your partner? Remember, your kids will wait while you make your marriage a priority, but your marriage won't wait until your kids grow up!

- *Are you—or should you be—in the empty nest stage?* Are you sandwiched between adult children, grandchildren and aging parents? While this may be a difficult stage of family life, you need to continue to invest in your marriage and focus on each other. Unfortunately, when we entered the empty nest stage, we went from a child-focused marriage to a ministry-focused marriage. While our children were growing up, we limited overnight engagements, knowing that we could freely travel and speak together when our sons left home. But just after entering our empty nest stage, we accepted too many speaking engagements and signed too many book contracts. We were caught in a ministry-focused marriage and had to really work to make it partner-focused!

Wherever you are, choose to focus on your partner. Take a few minutes and talk about how you demonstrate a partner focus in the following areas:

- *In your role as a parent:* Do you continually put your children first?

- *In work and home responsibilities:* If you have a choice to spend thirty minutes with your mate or complete a low-priority project, which would you choose?

🔖 *In relationships with others:* Who is a higher priority in your life, your friends or your spouse?

🔖 *In your leisure activities:* Do you seek out activities that you can do together?

Then talk about how you can face life's challenges together as partners. Trust us, your marriage will grow strong as you focus on your partner. You can stay close when you focus on helping each other. Any help we offer our mate helps our marriage partnership. Any pain, hurt, insult; any lack of support or faithfulness; any failure to help our spouse will reflect back on our marriage. You can be the most positive, reinforcing person in your partner's life and your partner in yours if you are willing to look out for the interests of each other.

Turn the Ordinary
Into Encouragement

"But encourage one another daily,
as long as it is called Today."

HEBREWS 3:13

"Sweet is the scene where genial friendship plays the pleasing game of interchanging praise."

OLIVER WENDELL HOLMES

Everyone needs encouragement, and healthy marriages thrive on it. So our best advice is to develop the encouragement habit. It's easy to do and doesn't require any heroic deeds or anything out of the ordinary. You can develop the encouragement habit by simply doing the ordinary with a special twist.

Other words for encouragement are helpfulness, comfort, support and assurance–all are great marriage vitamins. So any way–even simple, ordinary ways–we encourage each other will help to build a better relationship.

How can you turn the ordinary into encouragement? We asked the participants in our Marriage Alive Seminars to tell us how they encourage their spouses and how they like to be encouraged. Here are some of their best answers:

- Encouragement is listening to my spouse and not always trying to fix something.

- Encouragement is leaving a voice mail with a kiss.

- Encouragement is doing the dishes when it's not your turn.

- Encouragement is being the first to offer to change stinky diapers.

- Encouragement is leaving the porch light on.

- Encouragement is mowing the lawn without being asked.

- Encouragement is exercising together.

- Encouragement is saying, "Go back to sleep, Honey; I'll get the baby."

- Encouragement is giving a hug.

- Encouragement is taking an afternoon nap together.

- Encouragement is turning off the television and saying, "Let's talk!"

Now it's your turn. Here is your daily encouragement prescription. Turn the ordinary into encouragement. Think of one way today you can:

- Help your mate.

- Give your mate comfort.

- Support your mate.

- Assure your mate of your love.

Go on and encourage your mate today. It's the best way we know to develop the encouragement habit!

Think Before You Buy

"Therefore I tell you, do not worry about your life, what you will eat or drink; or about your body, what you will wear. Is not life more important than food, and the body more important than clothes?"

MATTHEW 6:25

"A man may have more money than brains, but not for long."

ANONYMOUS

We've talked to too many struggling couples who are drowning in consumer debt. Often we hear, "We just don't know how it happened!" Usually it's not a big mystery. Their *"outgo"* was more than their *income*.

Others tell us how they just couldn't pass up such a good deal on the–you can fill in the blank–car, house, vacation, computer, golf clubs–oops, now we're meddling.

Well, it may date us, but our first really dumb financial decision was buying a set of encyclopedias. Supposedly we didn't buy them! We were chosen for a special promotion. Now, just how did they choose our door? Just out of college, Dave was a second lieutenant in the Army. We were living in El Paso, Texas, where Dave was in basic Air Defense training at Fort Bliss. At last we had a real (however meager) salary! But now $40 a month was going to pay for our "free" encyclopedias that would be so useful one day when Claudia taught school and, of course, our future children would jump up and down in their cribs with all the intellectual stimulation.

Dumb decision? YES! Useless? Not completely–they were a continual reminder to think before we buy in the future!

Do you buy before you think or think before you buy? It's much harder to keep perspective today than when we were in the Army. In our consumer-oriented society, people work full-time to convince us that we need more things. And the more we get the more we tend to want. Stop and think about this. Will you really feel deprived if you don't buy things you've never had in the first place?

Things, we are told, will make us sexy, beautiful, desirable and even slimmer. They will bring true love and happiness. All we need is a little plastic card and we can have it all–*now*. Hogwash! That's simply not true. Too many couples who have it all, materially, have miserable relationships and end up with broken marriages.

We are convinced that if you want to build a healthy relationship, invest time, not more money! Yet many try to fill the void in their relationships with empty hours at the mall walking aimlessly through stores buying unnecessary items that end up in garage sales. So before you head for the mall, consider the following questions. You may even want to jot them down on a card and take it with you to the mall.

- Is this an item I really need?

- Have I taken care of other financial obligations?

- Can I really afford it?

- Why do I want to buy this item? Is it greed or need? Am I trying to impress my friends?

When you answer these questions honestly, you should make wiser decisions. And if you don't have all the answers, our best advice is *don't buy.* The next time you're feeling blue, bored or empty, visit your favorite walking path instead of the mall! Invite your spouse along. You can call it a "financial savings date"! You may end up with more brains than money—and that could be very positive!

Keep Your Promises

"Let love and faithfulness never leave you; bind them around your neck, write them on the tablet of your heart."

PROVERBS 3:3

"To have and to hold from this day forward, for better, for worse, for richer, for poorer, in sickness and in health, to love and to cherish, till death do us part."

THE BOOK OF COMMON PRAYER

Do you remember promising to love each other until "death us do part"? Did the stars in your eyes block the reality that keeping this promise would require hard work on your part? Building a loving and enriched marriage is a lifelong job that requires much effort and sacrifice.

Unless you are really committed to keeping your vows, it's easy to give up when problems come along; anyone who's been married more than a few days knows that problems will surface. All marriages have problems, but a difference exists in those marriages that survive and those that don't: successful couples are committed to keeping their vows, growing together and working to solve each problem that arises.

"For better, for worse, for richer, for poorer, in sickness and in health...", the marital vows go beyond just sticking together. It's also a commitment to adapt to each other's changing needs and your changing circumstances. To build a vibrant, long-term marriage requires a willingness to grow and adapt all the days of your life. In one sense, you continually adjust and change to maintain the same loving, alive relationship.

Adapting to each other requires self-sacrifice, but if we

refuse to adapt, we will have only a mediocre marriage. Adapting means thinking of the other person and looking for ways to grow together. It means being each other's best friend–being that one person the other can always count on. What are you doing to adapt to your mate?

Take a few moments and reflect on your marriage. Jot down your answers to the following two questions, and over two cups of *café au lait,* share your answers with the one with whom you have chosen to spend the rest of your life.

1. In what ways have I changed over the years to adapt to my spouse?

2. In what ways do I presently need to adapt or change to continue to be a loving and faithful spouse?

You may find this is one exercise that you can write on the tablet of your heart.

Be a Marriage Mentor

"It was he who gave some to be apostles, some to be prophets, some to be evangelists, and some to be pastors and teachers, to prepare God's people for works of service, so that the body of Christ may be built up until we all reach unity in the faith and in the knowledge of the Son of God and become mature, attaining to the whole measure of the fullness of Christ."

EPHESIANS 4:11–13

"We view marriage mentors as the sleeping giant within the church, about to rise and offer immeasurable hope and help."

DRS. LES & LESLIE PARROTT

Would you like to be part of a movement that is revolutionizing marriages? Then start mentoring other couples! Nothing can encourage another couple like a seasoned couple who love each other and have a great relationship.

With the divorce rate soaring within the church, we can help turn the tide by investing in other marriages as we invest in our own. And we have a fun, easy way you can begin. You can join with us and others around the country who are discovering the secrets of building a great marriage by dating their spouses! How? By organizing your own dating club called Couples' Nights Out™. As you date your spouse you will encourage other couples to do the same.

Your local church is a great place to begin. Our culture has become so transient, but we believe the church can fill the gap and for many can be the extended family for the twenty-first century. Your church can help by starting Couples' Nights Out.

Couples' Nights Out is just that, a night out for couples to have time to build their marriages and to enrich their relationships. As we work with couples across the country, they continually tell us, "We want to work on our marriage, but we don't have the time, money, child care providers or energy. Besides, we wouldn't know what to do or where to go!"

The Couples' Nights Out concept responds to this dilemma. Often after our Marriage Alive Seminar, churches offer follow-up growth groups, and occasionally they will provide free child care once a month so couples can go out on a date. Here is a chance to combine both fun dates and marriage enrichment skills.

At each Couples' Night Out, couples watch a short video-date launch where we introduce a dating theme based on a marital skill from our Marriage Alive Seminar. Then we actually launch the couples on their date by giving each couple the gift of time alone to experience their own "great date"! We suggest one and a half hours as an ideal time–long enough to have a real date but not long enough to go to a movie. Giving couples the gift of time alone together allows them the opportunity to apply biblical principles to their relationships. As we have worked with couples in the church over the past twenty-five years, we have observed over and over that doing what we know–not knowing what to do–is the fundamental dating problem. Couples' Nights Out gives husbands and wives the opportunity to immediately apply what they are learning. And the positive peer pressure from other couples helps them stay on course. That's what mentoring is all about.

For more information on how to start Couples' Nights Out, write to us or visit us on the World Wide Web at marriagealive.com. You can join the mentoring revolution and help other couples make their marriage a promise for life!

RESOURCES BY
DAVID AND CLAUDIA ARP

BOOKS

Love Life for Parents

10 Great Dates to Revitalize Your Marriage

The Second Half of Marriage

Where the Wild Strawberries Grow

The Love Book

52 Dates for You and Your Mate

The Ultimate Marriage Builder

The Marriage Track

60 One-Minute Family Builders Series

VIDEO CURRICULUM

10 Great Dates to Revitalize Your Marriage

PEP (Parents Encouraging Parents) Groups for Moms

PEP Groups for Parents of Teens

AUDIO PAGES

The Second Half of Marriage

SEMINARS FOR BUILDING BETTER RELATIONSHIPS

The Marriage Alive Seminar

The Arps' most demanded seminar is an exciting, fun-filled approach to building thriving marriages. Some of the topics included in this six-hour seminar are prioritizing your marriage, finding unity in diversity, communicating your feelings, processing anger and resolving conflict, cultivating spiritual intimacy and having an intentional marriage.

10 Great Dates
Couples' Nights Out

Let the Arps help you launch your own Couples' Nights Out with this one-evening kick-off. Then follow this fun evening with ten great dates launches based on their popular book and video resource, *10 Great Dates to Revitalize Your Marriage*, which will help spark romance with memory-making evenings, built on key marriage-enriching themes. A simple way to initiate an ongoing marriage enrichment program for your church or group.

The Second Half of Marriage

Based on their national survey of long-term marriages and their Gold Medallion Award winning book, *The Second Half of Marriage*, the Arps reveal eight challenges that all long-term marriages face and give practical strategies for surmounting each. Topics include choosing a partner-focused marriage, renewing the couple friendship, focusing on the future and growing together spiritually.

The Parenting Seminar

The Arps share the secret of how to *regroup, release, relate* and *relax!* Learn how to develop positive family dynamics, add fun and focus to family life and build supportive relationships with other parents. This seminar will help you prepare for the adolescent years and then actually enjoy them!

To schedule the Arps for a Seminar
or other speaking engagement contact:
Alive Communications
1465 Kelly Johnson Blvd., Suite 320
Colorado Springs, CO 80920
Phone: (719)260-7080 Fax: (719)260-8223

ABOUT THE AUTHORS

David and Claudia Arp are the founders and directors of Marriage Alive International, a marriage and family education ministry. The Arps conduct seminars across the United States and Europe.

David received a MSW from the University of Tennessee and Claudia holds a bachelor's degree in Home Economics Education from the University of Georgia. They have been featured on "CBS This Morning," "The 700 Club," and "On Main Street," produced by the Lutheran Hour. They host *The Family Workshop*, which is aired daily on over two-hundred radio stations.

The Arps have been married for thirty-five years and have three married adult sons and five grandchildren. They live in Knoxville, Tennessee.

FOR MORE INFORMATION:

About Marriage Alive
Couple Enrichment Resources
contact:
Marriage Alive International, Inc.
P.O. Box 31408, Knoxville, TN 37930

Phone: (423)691-8505
Fax: (423)691-1575

www.marriagealive.com